Judo for Beginn

KW-482-009

The author holds the grade of 5th Dan and is a Senior
Examiner of the British Judo Association. He was also one
of the coaches appointed for the Collett, Dickenson, Pearce
and Partners – London Judo Society Olympic Prospects
Venture which was designed to coach juniors, both boys and
girls, to the standard required to join the British Judo
Association Olympic and International squads. He is a
former British International and winner of the National
Judo Tournament.

ERIC DOMINY

Judo for Beginners

Illustrated by Peter Johnson

DRAGON
Granada Publishing

Dragon Books
Granada Publishing Ltd.
8 Grafton Street, London W1X 3LA

Published by Dragon Books 1983
A Dragon Original

Copyright © Autumn Publishing Ltd,
10 Eastgate Square, Chichester 1983

British Library Cataloguing in Publication Data
Autumn Publishing Ltd
Judo for Beginners
I. Title
823'.914[F]   PR6063.E8

ISBN 0-583-30629-2

Reproduced, printed and bound in Great Britain by
Hazell Watson & Viney Limited, Aylesbury

Set in Times

All rights reserved. No part of this publication may
be reproduced, stored in a retrieval system, or
transmitted, in any form, or by any means, electronic,
mechanical, photocopying, recording or otherwise,
without the prior permission of the publishers.

This book is sold subject to the conditions that it
shall not, by way of trade or otherwise, be lent,
re-sold, hired out or otherwise circulated
without the publisher's prior consent in any
form of binding or cover other than that in
which it is published and without a similar
condition including this condition being imposed
on the subsequent purchaser.

Contents

WHAT IS JUDO?

Judo is an ideal activity for just about everyone. It is not only a fighting sport which, therefore, instils initiative and self-confidence but is also a really first class exercise. It comes as a surprise to many people to find that there are very few injuries – far fewer than occur in the average football team. Students are not only taught how to throw their partner but also to look after him or her whilst they do it. All good clubs insist that their students keep themselves and their judo clothing spotlessly clean.

A common fallacy is that knowledge of a few simple judo tricks will make you invincible against almost all attacks. This is nonsense. Although judo training does provide a good basis for most effective self-defence, self-defence itself is a separate art and is usually taught outside the judo class. The fascination of judo is that you never stop learning. There is a counter to every movement and every counter can itself be countered. There will never be a stage in your judo career when you will not be able to look back and think of some thing which you have learned or discovered during the previous six months.

That strength does not matter is another general misconception. This is completely false and is the reason that judo competitions are arranged in weight categories. If the bodyweight and strength are more or less equal, the more skilful contestant is almost certain to win.

But if one of the contestants is lighter than his opponent he will need superior skill even to stand a chance of overcoming the heavier man. Yet it is not unknown for a lighter, more skilful exponent to overcome his heavier adversary as skill always provides a greater chance of victory than strength and weight.

PROMOTION IN GRADE

The examination system for promotion in grade is similar in most countries. The national association appoints examiners, and promotion in grade depends on a combination of technical knowledge, knowledge of theory and contest ability. Juniors are permitted to take part in one examination every three months and seniors in one every two months. There are special arrangements for promotion to and within the Dan grade. Every effort is made to ensure that students meet opponents of approximately the same grade, weight and age.

THE RULES OF JUDO

In this book I am including only an outline of the rules. Just sufficient for the reader to understand what the sport of judo is all about and how contests are conducted. It is absolutely essential that anyone taking part in the sport of judo, even if he has no contest ambitions, should thoroughly understand the rules, particularly those which relate to forbidden actions.

Knowledge of the contest rules is as important during grading examinations or even a club training session as in a major competition.

I must make it clear that whilst judo should not be a dangerous sport it can be made so by ignorance of the rules. In any case it is disappointing to lose a contest which should have been won because of lack of knowledge of a technical point. Most clubs teach the rules during their training sessions but it is really the responsibility of each student to study the rules of his sport. Copies of the rules can be obtained from your own club or the national association. Any points which are not clear should be discussed with your club or class instructor.

HOW CONTESTS ARE WON

The same rules apply to both senior and junior judo contests with the exception that juniors are not usually allowed to apply neck locks (**Shime-waza**) or arm locks (**Kansetsu-waza**). Certainly such locks are forbidden to the younger children.

Contests are won by the scoring of one point (**Ippon**) or two half points (**Waza-ari**) or a larger number of minor scores than your opponent.

The scoring in judo is as follows:-

Ippon A full point. Gained by throwing your opponent on his back with skill and impetus or by holding him on his back for 30 seconds (see section on **Osaekomi-waza** Holding techniques).

Waza-ari Almost a full point from a throw which is not quite good enough to score **Ippon** or for a hold of 25 seconds or more which cannot be maintained for the full 30 seconds. Two **Waza-ari** equal **Ippon** and win the contest.

Yuko For a throw not quite good enough to score **Waza-ari** or a hold which is maintained for 20 seconds or more but not for 25 seconds. However, no matter how many **Yukos** you score, they cannot add up to a **Waza-ari**. If no **Ippon** or **Waza-ari** is scored the contestant with the greatest number of **Yukos** wins.

Koka Almost **Yuko**. Like **Yuko** these cannot add up to a higher score. They are won by a throwing technique not quite good enough to score **Yuko** or for holding on the ground for over 10 seconds but less than 20 seconds. A contest is decided on **Kokas** if no higher score has been awarded.

STARTING JUDO

When you walk into the **Dojo** (practice hall) or your club for the first time you will see that the floor is covered with mats. These are usually green with a three foot (one metre) wide red mat surrounding them. The red mats warn students that they are getting close to the edge. These mats are kept spotlessly clean and no-one ever steps on to them without first removing his shoes. The mats are there to protect the students from injury but to the beginner they always appear very hard. This is because mats that are soft enough to allow the feet to sink into them are almost certain to cause injury and you cannot learn good judo unless you have a firm, fast surface upon which to move.

You will have obtained your judo suit (**Judogi**). This consists of a reinforced cotton jacket, light cotton trousers and a belt. All these are white and it is expected that you will keep the jacket and trousers clean. A different coloured belt is worn around the waist, indicating your grade. Many judo black belts wear the belt which came with their first judo suit although they have now dyed it black. You will have to learn how to tie up your trousers and belt – your instructor will show you how to do this. Men and women wear identical outfits except that the women wear a T-shirt or something similar under their jacket.

UKEMI – BREAKING YOUR FALL

Before you learn any throws it is essential that you are taught to fall correctly. Breakfalling, although it can be spectacular, is not particularly difficult to learn. In fact the first hour should take a complete beginner to the stage where he can fall safely if thrown with care and consideration, and in addition can perform one or two throws on an unresisting partner and one

Osaekomi technique (hold down). The principles of breakfalling are:

1 Fall with the body relaxed.

2 Take the fall with the body curled up and rolling. Do not stop the roll with your bottom or shoulders – the result of falling with your back straight.

3 Beat the mat with the underside of your lower arm just before your body lands on the mat. The arm must be relaxed and beat at an angle of about 45° from your body.

4 It is important that you beat with the arm so that it swings past your side from front to rear. This is more effective than beating from the centre of your body outwards. Try this for yourself whilst standing up. The first method allows the arm to swing well back just as if you were walking, whilst if you use the second method the arm stops more or less level with your body as your shoulder joint stops the movement. Obviously the first way allows much more flexibility and is much safer.

This may sound complicated but you will not have much difficulty when you receive a practical lesson.

You will see variations, such as using the feet to check the fall, being used by experienced club members. Do not attempt this. Keep to basic methods of falling in the early stages.

You can be thrown only in three directions, backwards, to the side or forwards. You are very unlikely to be thrown forwards in the early stages of your judo career so I will keep to the backward and sideways fall.

The backward breakfall
To practise squat down on your heels with your head tucked in and your arms above your head (*see illustration 1*). Now roll backwards gently at the same time bringing your arms down to beat the mat (*illustration 2*). The roll back should be

Illustration 1

smooth and relaxed so that you do not strike the mat with your bottom, back, shoulders or head. The arms should be kept straight but relaxed, beating from the shoulder so that you do not hurt your elbow on the mat. Keep your fingers together, as single fingers can easily be damaged.

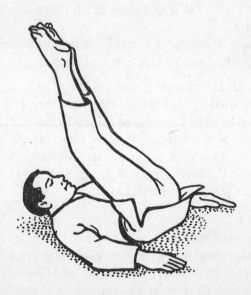

Illustration 2

The sideways breakfall

This is the most common fall in judo and as most judomen throw right handed you are most likely to have to fall on your left side. However you must practise falling on both sides.

Squat down with your head tucked in and raise your right arm upwards across your face (*illustration 3*). Now roll

Illustration 3

backwards and to your right beating the mat with your right arm as you do so. The arm beats at about 45° to your body (*illustration 4*). Try this both to left and right.

As you become more proficient get down on your hands and knees. Get a partner to stand at your right side. By putting his arm under your body he grips your left sleeve (*illustration 5*). Now by pulling on that sleeve he turns you over so that you have to breakfall by beating the mat with your right arm. Try this slowly at first and then, as you find you are beating the mat with your arm before your body lands, increase the speed.

Finally a partner or instructor will throw you gently from

Illustration 4

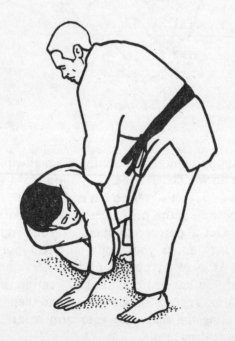

Illustration 5

the standing position so that you get the feel of an actual throw.

THROWING YOUR PARTNER

It is essential that beginners are taught to fall and do not lose confidence. Whenever you throw you should retain your hold on your opponent's jacket with the inside hand (left hand for right handed throws as shown in illustration) and help him to fall (*illustration 6*). In this way no beginner takes a heavy fall and loses confidence. When you are practising your throws a crash mat is very useful to take your partner's falls.

Illustration 6

BASIC POSTURE

Posture is very important because every time you move you sacrifice your balance and posture and give your opponent an opportunity of throwing you. However, by relaxed and well balanced movement this danger can be greatly reduced. The ideal basic posture is to stand with the feet about shoulder width apart; the knees should be relaxed and slightly bent as should the ankles. Your trunk should be upright (*illustration 7*). If you watch judo contests you will often see defensive

Illustration 7

postures adopted in which the competitors crouch with the body bent forward and the arms straight. Never take up this position as from it you cannot learn judo. Not only have you no control from this position but you are seriously restricting your breathing. Although you should keep your feet flat on the mat as you move about, keep your balance on the balls of your feet.

BASIC HOLD ON THE JACKET

There is no fixed hold on the jacket although certain holds are forbidden by the rules. There is one hold which is used for beginners in just about every judo club. Stand facing your partner. With your right hand grip his left lapel at about the level of your own chest. Your left hand grasps his right sleeve below his elbow (*illustration 8*). A little experimenting will

Illustration 8

show you that as you turn to your left (the usual turn to attack by a right handed judo player) you have a strong pull with your left arm and as your turn develops you can build up considerable driving or pushing power with your right arm.

MOVEMENT ABOUT THE MAT

Nothing is more likely to get you thrown than careless movement on the mat. Trial and error will soon show you that if you bring your feet close together you can be pushed over in any direction. If you actually cross your feet, and it is only too easy to do this, you will almost fall over without any help from your opponent. Finally if you get your feet too wide apart your balance is easily upset to your front and backwards.

Illustration 9

What then is the answer? You must try and maintain your basic posture as you move about, keeping your balance evenly distributed on both feet. If you step forward, say with your left foot, you should keep your feet about shoulder width apart as it passes your right (*illustration 9*). Immediately the left foot is put back on the mat place your weight again evenly on both feet. Your knees should be kept relaxed and slightly bent as you move.

If you are moving sideways, say to your left, move your left foot to the left first – not too far – and then bring your right foot up to its basic position about shoulder width from it. Again keep the knees bent and relaxed and with the weight distributed between your feet (*illustration 10*).

As you become more experienced you will find that most judo movements are made from the hips. If you wish to step forward with your left foot advance your left hip. The foot must come as well because it is attached to the hip. The movement might sound much the same when I describe it but by moving the hip the foot is kept beneath the knee which improves your balance.

RANDORI (FREE PRACTICE)

Randori really means free fighting but this form of 'fighting' has no connection with contests. In judo clubs all techniques are practised by taking part in **Randori**. The students pair up and try out their techniques. Grade and age do not matter because the older and more skilful help their partners and should never take advantage of them. The object is to improve your techniques and perhaps attempt variations and forms of bluff. Every so often you change partners so that you are getting practice against people of different size, strength and weight.

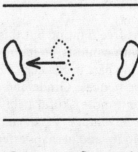

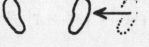

Illustration 10

TACHI-WAZA THROWING TECHNIQUES – BASIC PRINCIPLES.

1 *To the opponent's front*

The theory of judo techniques is simple and easily understood. Unfortunately what is easy to understand is often very difficult indeed to carry out. The thrower has to maintain his own balance and posture whilst attacking a strongly resisting opponent. Often he has to turn his back on that opponent, usually whilst balancing himself on one leg. Easy?

What then are the principles of **Tachi-waza**? You have to overcome your opponent's resistance whilst bringing into play all your own strength and power against his weakest points.

The opponent's main defensive strength is in his arms. As long as he can hold you out – often with stiff arms – you will find it very difficult to bring off a successful attack.

If you attack straight into the opponent's straight arms they will be too strong for you. You must move so that you exert your force against them sideways where they are weak or in the direction in which he is pushing or pulling. Sometimes both (*see illustration 17 on page 33*). The initial requirement when you attack is to tilt your opponent forward on his toes and bring his chest fairly close to your own. This is very difficult if he takes up a strong straight arm defensive posture but you must attempt to do it. To attack the opponent's arms in the direction in which they are weak applies to all throws and also to groundwork. It is very important but I have not, because of shortage of space, mentioned it in my description of every technique. Now try it for yourself. Adopt a normal posture and take the normal hold but get your partner to straighten his arms fairly strongly. If you try to get close to him by stepping in towards him you may manage to get your feet and hips close but his stiff arms hold the top half of your body out from him. If you attempt to turn to your left to throw in this position you will lose your balance backwards.

Now start from the basic posture once more, holding each other's jackets, and again get your partner to stiffen his arms. This time take your left leg backwards behind you in a circular movement. Imagine your body as a geometrical compass. Your right foot is the point which will be the centre of the circle whilst your left foot must be thought of as the pencil. Without changing the position of your right foot begin to make a circle with your left (*illustration 11*). Replace it on the mat when you have turned a little further than sideways to him – about 50° to 60°. The actual amount of turn depends on which throw you are attempting.

Although I have to describe the movement piece by piece all the movements have to be made at the same time. Look at the basic hold on the jacket once more. Your hands are in front of your chest and as you turn they must remain in this position.

As your left hip and foot is taken back, your chest turns as well, taking your arms round too. During your turn pull back and round with your left hand and push to your left, round and upwards with your right. Note the angle of the wrists in the illustrations. You will see that by moving in this way your left hand pulls the opponent's right arm outwards and past your left shoulder, and your right drives his left arm sideways and upwards. In this way both arms are attacked sideways where they are weak and your opponent has his balance completely destroyed.

2 *To the opponent's rear*

When you want to throw your opponent backwards the problems are much the same as attacking an opponent to his front. You walk straight into his defensive arms as you attempt to move close enough to him to make your throw. A typical example is an attempt to attack with **O-soto-gari** (major outer reaping). The throw is described on page 30. As you step forward with your left foot intending to place it

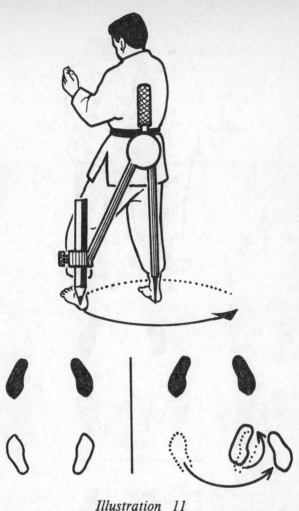

Illustration 11

outside his right foot, you are blocked by the opponent's right arm. To attempt to complete the throw once you have been blocked is to ensure that a successful counter attack can be made against you. As usual the stiff arm defence must be overcome.

23

Illustration 12

To do this, step in, but place your left foot about 12 inches (30 cm) to the left of your opponent's right foot (*illustration 12*). As you do so pull his right arm outwards and upwards and at the same time turn your chest a little to your left. This pushes his right arm outwards so that you move inside it as you move close to him.

3 *To the opponent's side*
Attacking to the opponent's side is difficult and hardly comes into the scope of an introduction to judo for beginners. However it has been described on page 27 for the **Tai-otoshi** throw.

4 *Principles applicable to all throws*
I suggest you read these principles and then as you study the throws in this book read them again many times. Each time you read them you will understand them more.

As it is essential to bring all your power into use when you attempt a throw, you must always be in a position from which you can drive your body in the direction in which you intend to throw your opponent. There are a few general rules (to which there are, of course, always exceptions) which will help you do this. You will see these in use when you look at the illustrations of the throws.

1 Always place the foot upon which you have your weight and balance pointing in the direction in which you wish your opponent to fall.

2 Always keep the knee of the foot upon which you have your weight well bent, with the knee above or even in front of your toes. This is essential if you are to keep your balance and adds power to your throws.

3 Keep your back hollowed as you attack. Do not bend forward as you decrease your effective power if you do this.

4 Usually the throwing leg, the one on which you do not have your weight, is kept straight or straightens during the throw. Do not attack with a hooked leg, as this is not effective. The straight leg permits the power of your hips to be brought into play against your opponent. There are several exceptions to this.

5 You cannot throw your opponent, unless you are strong enough to lift him, if you are standing in the place where he should fall. This is why you have to turn in so many of the throws. Look at **Hiza-guruma** – the knee wheel throw on page 32. If you attempt the throw whilst you are standing directly in front of your opponent he cannot fall because your own body is in the way. This is why you move your right foot to your right when attacking with the knee wheel throw. The step gets your body out of his way and also allows your body to turn through a far greater angle.

6 Note that sometimes you get out of the way of his fall by lowering your body. Examples are shoulder and hips throws and especially the sacrifice throws. In these techniques you lower your hips so that the opponent can be thrown over them by leverage and the turn of your hips.

7 Throughout this book I have talked about turning your body to attack an opponent to his front. I must make it clear that you make your turn by moving your hips and having turned sufficiently you replace your left foot on the mat. Your turn, however, does not cease when your left foot is on the mat but goes on by continuing to turn your hips. This constant turning of the hips in a clockwise circle should continue until the throw is complete. This will become clear as you attempt the throws.

ASHI WAZA (LEG TECHNIQUES OR THROWS)

Leg throws are those in which you use your leg to throw your opponent. The leg may be used either as a platform over which he might fall or as a lever to take his leg or legs from under him.

Tai-otoshi (The body drop throw)

This throw is usually used against an opponent who is holding you away with stiff arms. It is easier if he steps forward with his right foot, although it does not matter if he keeps it back. Take your left hip and leg back in a circle and replace it on the mat when it is approximately in front of his left foot. Your knee should be bent and your left foot turned slightly to your left. Immediately your left foot is replaced on the mat stretch your right leg out sideways to your right. As you commence to withdraw your left hip and leg you should turn your hips, chest, arms and head all to the left in exactly the same circle as that taken by your hips. Your left arm pulling and your right pushing and lifting. In this way your opponent will be drawn straight to his front to fall over your outstretched right leg (*illustration 13*). The fact that you are turning in a circle will ensure that he falls on to his back.

Your outstretched right leg should be turned so that contact is made with the mat with the underside of the toes, and the ankle and knee turned so that they will bend if your opponent falls across your leg. This way, as you can see in the illustration, no injury will be caused.

You will note that I said that the right leg should be stretched out sideways. No effort should be made to take the leg back to trap your opponent's right foot. If you do this not only are you likely to kick his shin which might injure both of you but, more important, as you move the leg back it throws your weight backwards and stops your turn to your left. This takes a great deal of power out of your throw.

Strictly **Tai-otoshi** is a hand throw although I have included it amongst the leg throw techniques. This is because although the throw should be made by the power of the turn of your hips and the drive of your arms and hands – a hand

Illustration 13

throw – more often your opponent is thrown over your outstretched leg. Therefore it is included in the leg throw group.

A variation to **Tai-otoshi** (The body drop throw)
Your opponent is moving sideways to his right. On this occasion you step to your left as he moves to his right and pivot to your left on your left foot bringing your right hip and leg across the front of his body, replacing it on the mat outside his right foot. If, as you bring your right leg across, you turn

your hips and body in an anti-clockwise circular movement, your left arm will pull his right arm sideways (to his right) and your right arm will drive his left arm to his right and upwards. He will be tilted over the right outside edge of his right foot and thrown over your outstretched leg (*illustration 14*). Note that your turn must be made by pivoting your hips. If you try to turn by moving your right hip towards your opponent you will be blocked by his straightened left arm.

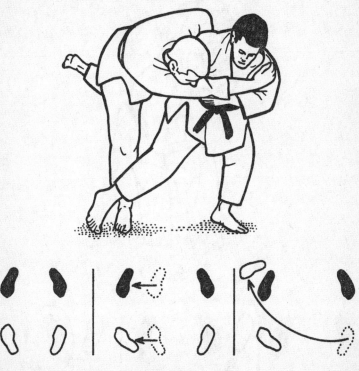

Illustration 14

O-soto-gari *(Major outer reaping throw)*

This is a throw to the opponent's rear. It can be used against a static, defensive opponent who is holding you out with stiff arms. With your left hand pull his right arm outwards and towards you. It also helps if the pull is a little upwards. Your right hand also lifts a little and pulls towards you. As you move your arms, glide your left foot forward along the mat,

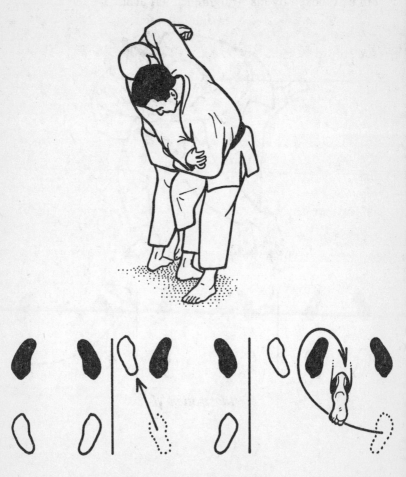

Illustration 15

replacing it when your toes are about level with the opponent's right heel and about 12 inches (30 cms) to the left of his foot (*look at illustration 12 again*).

As you advance your foot you must keep your weight over it and your knee bent so that your head and shoulders are above your toes. Your back should be hollowed. In this way you exert all your weight forward and cannot be pushed back off balance.

At this stage bring your right hip and leg forward and in a circular movement taking your leg past the outside of his right leg and behind it (*illustration 15*). Now driving your head and trunk down and forward thrust your leg back from the hip. As the leg straightens it will make contact with his leg behind the thigh and reap him off the mat, throwing him on his back (*illustration 16*). As the throw takes effect your body, from head to right toes, should be in a straight line parallel to the ground. At exactly the same time that you thrust your hip back you drive downwards with your arms aiming at a point just behind his right heel. The effect is sudden and can result in a very heavy fall and the victim can easily strike the mat hard with the back of his head.

Illustration 16

To practise the throw get someone to stand behind your partner and support and hold him up as you attempt the technique. In this way he will not actually be thrown and you can take turns to attack without taking a series of heavy falls.

Hiza-guruma (The knee wheel throw)

This is another throw which is effective against an opponent who adopts a defensive posture and holds you out with his arms. Step to your right and a little back with your right foot turning it to the left as you do so. You must take your hip back as well so that it remains over your foot. Your right knee must bend for balance as you turn. As you are moving the foot turn your hips and chest to the left (anti-clockwise) pulling with your left hand and driving in the same direction with your right. Once again it is important that your arms turn him in the same arc as that taken by your hips. If you push him away your throw will fail and he should be able to counterthrow you. Immediately your right foot is back on the ground bring the sole of your left foot up against his right leg just below his knee. As your turn continues he will be thrown over your foot to the mat (*illustration 17*).

Note how your step to the right at the beginning of the throw allows you to attack his arms to their side as you turn. It is important that the sole of your left foot must only be *placed* against the opponent's leg. If you push or kick, not only might you damage his knee but you cannot turn your hips anti-clockwise and push with your foot at the same time. It is equally important that you use the sole of the foot. Not only will you hurt your opponent if you use the edge of the foot but doing this will turn your leg and reduce the power deriving from your hips. Your left leg must be kept straight, because if you bend it you will also prevent the power of your hips being used through the foot and lessen the distance you can reach.

It is worth noting that should your opponent be standing

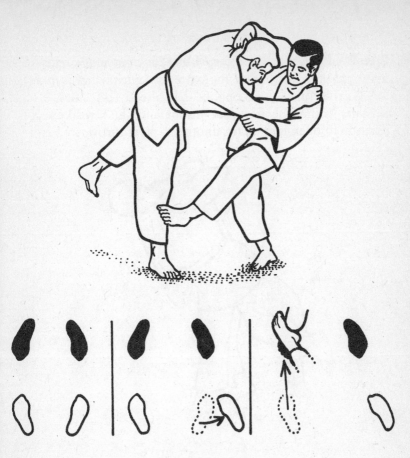

Illustration 17

upright instead of holding you out in a defensive position it is
necessary to step back as well as to your right with your right
foot as you attack. Unless you do this you will be too close to
him and find it impossible to bring your left foot into position
for the throw. In fact this is probably the wrong throw to use
against an upright free moving opponent. **Sasae-tsurikomi-
ashi** – the drawing ankle throw (*page 52*) – is a better choice of
throw for this situation.

O-uchi-gari (The major inner reaping throw)

Like **O-soto-gari** this is a throw to your opponent's rear. In my opinion this is one of the more difficult throws in judo, but it is useful if your opponent is already off balance or perhaps you want to upset his balance and weaken his position to open him up for another type of throw.

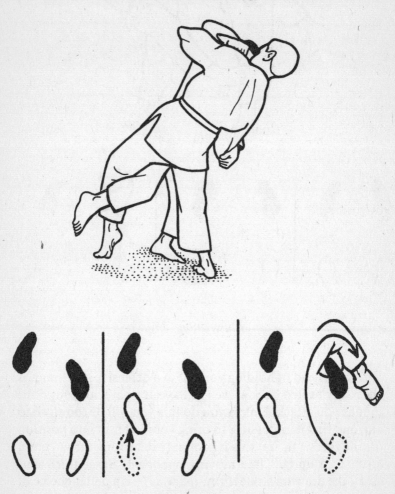

Illustration 18

The throw is best used against an opponent who is in a defensive posture, knees bent and arms straight. As you are going to throw him to his rear you have to get fairly close to him, so it is better to attack the leg which is closest to you. Imagine he is standing in his defensive position with his left leg advanced. Step in towards him with your left foot, turning it a little to your right as you do so and bending your left knee. Do not forget to advance your knee and hips at the same time. As you step in, turn your chest a little to your right and with your arms pull him slightly upwards and to your right. Your left arm will therefore push his right arm to your right and your right arm will pull and lift in the same direction – you are therefore attacking his defensive arms sideways.

Now bring your right leg in between his legs and by moving it in a clockwise circle take it behind the opponent's left leg. You should make contact with the bottom of your thigh just above or behind his knee (*illustration 18*). The rest of the throw is very like **O-soto-gari** (major outer reaping) on page 30.

You straighten your right leg, driving it back with your hip, and thrust your head and trunk downwards so that your body is straight from the toes of your right foot to the top of your head and parallel to the ground. As you do this you drive downwards with your arms aiming at a point just behind the point where his left heel rested before your attack.

Please note that this throw can result in a violent fall in which your opponent might hit his head on the mat. In addition it is very easy for you to lose your balance and fall on to him. When you practise therefore get someone to support your partner by standing behind him to prevent him falling, or use a crash mat.

KOSHI-WAZA (HIP THROW TECHNIQUES)

Although all judo throws, in fact all judo movements, are based on movement of the hips, the actual throwing instrument is the foot, the leg or the controlled weight and movement of the body. In the hip throw series, however, the hip not only controls the direction of the throws and supplies the power, it is the actual part of the body over which the opponent is thrown. Most throws of the hip throw group are used against an opponent who is moving upright and freely or, and this is much more difficult, with a stiff arm defence which you must overcome completely. At this stage ignore the latter as it requires considerable skill.

O-goshi (The major hip throw)

This is one of the most popular throws with beginners, no doubt because it can be brought off with strength rather than skill. This is the worst possible reason for liking any throw – all throws must succeed as the result of the use of skill. If you concentrate on strength in the early stages you will never be any good at judo and you will soon reach the point where strength no longer succeeds. First use skill and then add strength when you know how to control it.

Your opponent is in a good upright stance and is prepared to move fairly freely about the mat. Whenever possible attack with **O-goshi** when he has advanced his right foot or you can manoeuvre him on to it. Use your arms to bring him forward so that if possible his balance is on his toes. As you do this take your left hip and leg back in an anti-clockwise direction moving the leg until you can replace it on the mat level with your right foot and pointing in the same direction. You will see that you have made a 180° turn and have your back to your opponent. Your knees should be well bent and your trunk should be upright. All your weight should be on your right foot. Do not hesitate to place your feet fairly wide apart as this improves your balance and powers your hips.

As you begin your turn pull hard with your left hand which must draw your opponent round you in the same circle as that taken by your hips. Your right hand releases its grip on the left lapel of his jacket and your right arm is pushed down to your side and then as you turn is placed round his waist where it may hold his belt. You will see that by moving your right arm down, his arm is also pulled downwards and from this position it is much more difficult for him to hold your arm out when you try to push it round his waist. Your right arm pulls him tight against you and lifts slightly. As you do this push your hips out to your right so that it is more difficult for your opponent to escape by moving round you.

Now you have your back to your opponent with your right arm round his waist lean forward over your left foot and he will be lifted off his feet and balanced on your hips (*illustration 19*). If you continue your anti-clockwise turn he will be rolled over your hips and he will fall to the mat on his back.

This throw is more difficult to use successfully if you are taller than your opponent. You should attempt to get your hips lower than his as you turn by bending your knees – never by bending your body at the hips.

Harai-goshi (The sweeping hip or sweeping loin throw)

A spectacular throw which is the author's favourite technique. It is very graceful and whilst the movement is similar to **O-goshi** (*page 36*) it is much more difficult because you have to stand on one leg to make the throw.

Whilst **Harai-goshi** can be used against a defensive opponent, this is difficult and best left to more advanced students. We will assume therefore that your opponent is upright and moving freely.

When your opponent has his feet level or perhaps his right foot slightly advanced draw him forwards and slightly

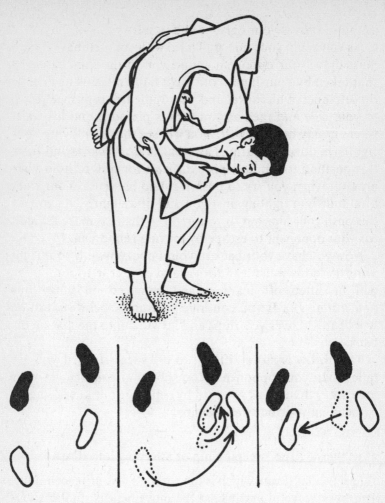

Illustration 19

upwards with your arms and by moving your left leg and hip
turn to your left (anti-clockwise). Replace your left foot on
the mat when it is between his feet – but about 2 feet (60 cms)
in front of them or about the same distance in front of his left
foot. As usual your left knee bends and the knee is over your
toes so that your balance is well forward. As you turn, your

left arm pulls his right arm round you and your right arm pushes his left arm upwards and round after your left arm. As you are turning this means that he is being pushed to his front. This applies to all the throws where you turn.

Now let us go back to the beginning. You take your right hip and leg back. As you place that foot on the mat, lift your right leg so that the knee is lifted outwards and upwards towards your opponent's right armpit. The knee must be taken upwards and out to your side and not just lifted forwards. Now leaning forward over your left knee, drive your head and shoulders downwards and thrust your right leg back turning the thigh anti-clockwise as you do so and allowing the leg to straighten. Once again you finish with your body and leg in a straight line parallel to the mat *(illustration 20)*.

If you have controlled your opponent with your arms you will find that as you lift your right leg he is pulled against your thigh. Now when you drive forward and turn the thigh he is actually lifted by the turning thigh which adds power to the throw.

Note how your right hip as it thrusts in the throw does not stop your hips turning.

I know that I have described the throw in several separate sections but you must appreciate that it is all one continuous movement and your hips should not cease their anti-clockwise turn until your opponent is thrown.

Harai-goshi (The sweeping hip throw to the side)

Either because your opponent is moving to his right or just because you wish to vary your tactics you decide to attack him with **Harai-goshi** to his right side. Step a little to your left with your left foot, turning it to your left as you do so and bring your right hip through to your left by pivoting your hips – not pushing the right hip forward – until you can bring your right thigh against his right side. Again you have lifted

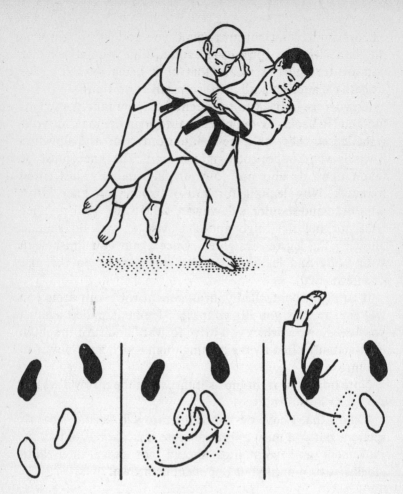

Illustration 20

your knee sideways, not forwards. You should have turned to
your left, about 45°. As you do this draw your opponent's
body forward and to his right by lifting and pulling with your
left hand and pushing to your left and driving upwards with
your right. The object is to tilt him on the outside edge of his
right foot and keep him close to you.

Now by driving the head and shoulders down and thrusting the hip back against the outside of his right thigh and straightening the leg, he is thrown over your thigh to the mat.

Although throws to the side are described in fewer words and probably appear more simple, this is actually not so. It is difficult to bring the right hip and leg through as you turn to your left without pushing it forward. If you move towards your opponent the throw will be blocked or countered. In addition it is easier to escape from a throw made in this direction.

Uchi-mata (The inner thigh throw)

This is almost certainly the most popular throw in judo. Not, in my opinion, because it succeeds more than any other throw but because it is very difficult to counter. It is not an easy throw and not suitable for beginners but I am including it because you are certain to see it used and may try it for yourself. It is better therefore that you know how it should be done. It is used against an opponent who takes up a very defensive stance and is easier if you can catch him moving forward or draw him forward.

Your opponent adopts a deeply defensive crouch. Pull him forwards and upwards with your arms and slide your left foot as far between his feet as possible. To do this you have to push your left hip well forward and bend the knee deeply so that you move under his stiff arms. You turn your left foot as far as you can to your own left before you replace it on the mat between his feet. Now bring your right thigh up between his legs and pivot hard to your left as you do so, straightening your left leg and driving your head and shoulders forward, thrusting your right hip back and straightening your throwing leg (*illustration 21*). Your body should now be parallel to the mat with your opponent stretched along your body and leg. By continuing to turn to your left you roll him off your thigh to the mat.

41

Illustration 21

You will see why it is essential to move in for the throw with a deeply bent left knee and then straighten the leg. If the knee is not bent in the initial attack you will not be able to get under his defensive arms. The leg must then be straightened because the opponent has to be lifted off his right leg. If he keeps that leg on the mat the throw will not work.

An alternative attack with Uchi-mata

An alternative means of getting in for the throw is much more like the other throws I have described. This time turn to your left by turning your hips and taking your left leg as far round as you can (see again illustration 11). A turn of at least 180° is required. As you turn, your left hand pulls his forward and upwards whilst your right arm drives in the same direction – to his front and upwards. Now the right leg is thrust between your opponent's legs and lifts as you turn and drive your head and shoulders downwards, continuing your turn as you do so.

You may find that you are still too far away from your opponent when you have brought your left leg round. In this case try a very difficult move. Maintain the forward pull and drive with your arms and hop into your opponent on your left foot. Now make the throw again.

Tsuri-komi-goshi (Drawing lifting hip throw)

A difficult but very graceful throw. **Tsuri-komi-goshi** is ideal for a contestant who is shorter than his opponent. The throw is suitable against an opponent who moves upright and freely and is very useful should an upright opponent lean back to resist an attack.

You turn in the usual way taking your left foot and hip back until it is level with your right. At this stage you have completed a turn of some 180° and finish with both knees deeply bent. As you turn your left arm draws him to his front and lifts slightly whilst your right arm drives him almost directly upwards and to his front (illustration 22). Now drive him forward on to your hips pushing your hips back into him as you do so. Because you still keep turning he falls on his back to the mat. He will be thrown almost directly to his front

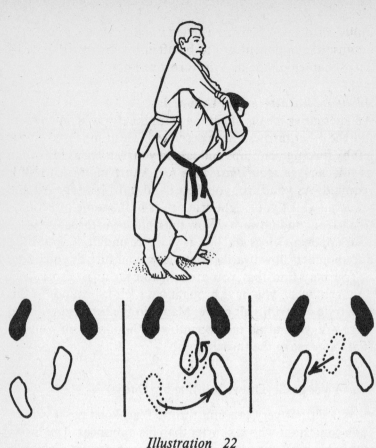

Illustration 22

over your hips. This can be a heavy throw and it is easy to lose your own balance and fall on him. Take care.

SEOI-WAZA (SHOULDER THROWS)

The shoulder throws are all graceful and spectacular but unless good technique is used they are all more open to counters than most throws. Although in theory the opponent should be thrown directly over the thrower's shoulder it is more usual for the throw to be made by continuing to turn and wind the victim round the attacker's shoulder. The danger of being countered arises when the attacker finds his shoulders too far away from the defender's chest and attempts to put the position right by lowering his right shoulder in an effort to get his shoulders underneath his opponent's defensive arms. At this stage he is very vulnerable to being thrown backwards.

I like these throws because of their power and effectiveness and possibly because of the extra excitement added by the danger of a counter attack. When you are learning take care and, if possible, use a crash mat.

Ippon-seoi-nage (The single sided shoulder throw)

This throw is best used against an opponent who is taller than you or at least about the same height. The movement required to make this throw is similar to **O-goshi** (the major hip throw, *page 36*) and they are particularly alike in that you have to change the grip of your right hand. The attack can be made when your opponent is fairly upright and preferably not holding you out too strongly with his arms. Pull him strongly to his front and a little upwards, particularly with your left hand, and at the same time take your left hip and leg back in a circular movement until you have your back to him. Your turn is about 180°. You should finish with your feet about 2 feet (60 cm) apart and your knees well bent. As you begin your turn release the grip of your right hand and bring the hand and arm in a circular movement downwards and then up under his right armpit. The circle continues as your arm comes round the opponent's right arm from the outside (*illustration 23*). At this stage beginners find it easier to grip their opponent's sleeve towards the end and immediately that right arm pulls strongly to the opponent's front and upwards in support of your left arm. This sounds very complicated but

45

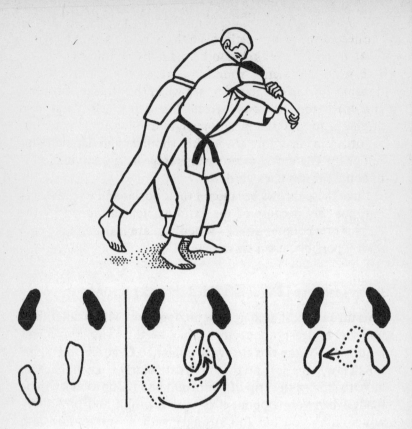

Illustration 23

is not too difficult and should become clear when you look at the illustration.

Continuing the anti-clockwise turn of your hips push your left hip back into your opponent; continue the pull to his front and upwards with your arms and he will be drawn over your right shoulder to the mat.

Take great care with this throw when you first try it because unless you continue to turn until he actually falls to the mat there is a danger of your losing your balance to your front and throwing your opponent on to his head.

There is one stage in this throw at which you may be in great danger of being countered. When you release the grip with your right hand and turn, you must lower your body by bending your knees otherwise you will fail to bring your right arm under your opponent's arm. If you cannot do this do not persist in your attack. The danger arises when, in an attempt to force your attack, you dip your right shoulder so that you can get your arm into position. As soon as this happens your opponent can throw you backwards.

Morote-seoi-nage (Two sided shoulder throw)

This shoulder throw is very similar to **Ippon-seoi-nage** except that you do not have to change the grip of your right hand. Again it is best used against an opponent who is upright and fairly relaxed and who is about your own height or taller. The danger of lowering your right shoulder in your attempt to make contact with your opponent is even greater than when you use **Ippon-seoi-nage** (*page 45*) so great care must be taken if you are not to be countered.

With both hands pull your opponent upwards and to his front at the same time taking your left foot and hip back in an anti-clockwise circle. Your turn should continue until your left foot is level with your right (at least 180°) and it should be replaced on the mat some 2 feet (60 cm) from your right (*see the foot prints in illustration 23*). The more you can turn the left foot to the left when you replace it on the mat the better. As you turn continue to drive the opponent to his front and a little upwards with your arms and move your right elbow in a circle downwards and then up under his right armpit. Do not lower the shoulder as you do this. The elbow lifts as well and not only adds to the upward pressure but also prevents him moving to his right and slipping out of the throw (*illustration 24*). Your continued turn and lift will drive your opponent over your right shoulder to the mat. It will help if you drive your left hip back into your opponent as you complete your

Illustration 24

turn. The danger of losing your balance is not as great in this throw as in **Ippon-seoi-nage** but take care otherwise your opponent might be thrown on his head.

Seoi-otoshi (The shoulder drop throw)

This is a variation of the shoulder throws which can be used against an opponent who is not as tall as you are or who is in a more defensive posture.

You are facing your opponent using the normal grip on his jacket. Again you have to make a turn of 180° or as close to this as possible so begin your turn taking your left hip back and round until you have your back to him and your left foot has been replaced on the mat. The left foot should be turned to the left as much as possible. Your knees should be bent. As your turn begins release your right hand grip on his jacket and take it in a circular movement down and then upwards

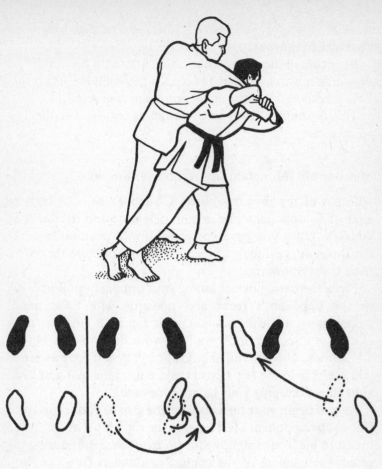

Illustration 25

bringing your arm underneath his upper arm and lean to your left front (*illustration 23 on page 46*). If you have turned your left foot sufficiently and have your balance forward so that your knees are above your toes, your continued turn with your hips and the drive to his front with your arms should tilt him forward. As you turn slide your right foot and hip back outside his right leg. This lowers your body (*illustration 25*).

As you continue your turn he will be hurled over your shoulder to the mat.

Note that in this throw your right upper arm goes under his right upper arm and there is no need to get under his armpit. This greatly reduces the danger of being countered.

This is another heavy throw which takes effect suddenly – so take care.

Yama-arashi (Mountain storm shoulder throw)

Another of my favourite throws, **Yama-arashi** can be used against an opponent who is both defensive and shorter than yourself. Once you have got yourself into position to make the throw it is difficult to counter mainly because the throw itself is very powerful.

From the basic posture facing your opponent pull strongly to the opponent's front and upwards with your hands commencing to withdraw your left hip in a circular, anti-clockwise direction until you have your back to him. As for all shoulder throws you should turn your left foot as far as you are able to the left as you replace it on the mat and bend your knees, keeping your balance forward.

As you begin your turn transfer the grip of your right hand from your opponent's left lapel to his right lapel and use it to thrust to his front and upwards (*illustration 26*). If during the general movement of the contest or **Randori** (practice) you can change the right hand grip before you commence the throw you will add strength to your attack because it will enable you to bring that hand into the throw at an earlier stage.

As your left foot is replaced on the mat continue the drive with your arms and the anti-clockwise turn of your hips and your opponent will be thrown over your right shoulder to the mat.

As you turn your right foot slides back until it is outside the right foot of your opponent, very like the movement used for

Tai-otoshi and **Seoi-otoshi**. At this stage it adds power to your throw if you lift your right leg from the mat (*illustration 26*), as in **Harai-goshi,** and reap. Continue to turn until your opponent falls. This is another powerful throw which can result in a heavy fall.

Illustration 26

ASHI-WAZA (FOOT THROWS AND TECHNIQUES)

You will see that the term **Ashi-waza** includes both leg and foot throws.

In this group of throws the opponent's ankle is attacked with the sole of your left foot. They are difficult throws and great care must be taken to use the sole of your foot so that neither you nor your opponent is injured. It is important in

51

most throws to keep the knee of the leg on which you stand bent as you throw and to attempt to keep the throwing leg straight. This is particularly important if ankle throws are to succeed. The throws are difficult but worth the trouble of the practice necessary to make them effective.

Sasae-tsurikomi-ashi (Lifting drawing ankle throw)

Your opponent's posture is upright. Wait until he moves his right foot forward or persuade him to do so by pulling him forward with your left arm. As he does so draw him forwards and upwards with your arms; at the same time step back and to your right with your right foot. As usual this foot movement is controlled from the hip, on this occasion the right hip. The right hip is taken back and to your right in an arc, the foot being turned to your left before it is replaced on the mat. At the same time the knee should be bent and the knee kept over your toes in order to keep your balance secure. Immediately your right foot is placed on the mat your left hip is withdrawn. Continue bringing your opponent to his front with your arms, and place the sole of your left foot against the front of his right shin as low down as possible; your leg being kept straight. Once again you will note how, as your left hip is withdrawn, the initial pull with your right hand becomes a push, driving him direct to his front (*illustration 27*).

You can see how the throw gets its name – the lifting drawing ankle throw. You lift him and bring him forward with your arms drawing his ankle forward on to the sole of your foot to make the throw.

Okuri-ashi-barai (The sweeping ankle throw)

This is a very effective throw but only after a great deal of practice because however well you understand the theory of the throw, and however strong you are, **Okuri-ashi-barai** cannot work unless your timing is almost perfect.

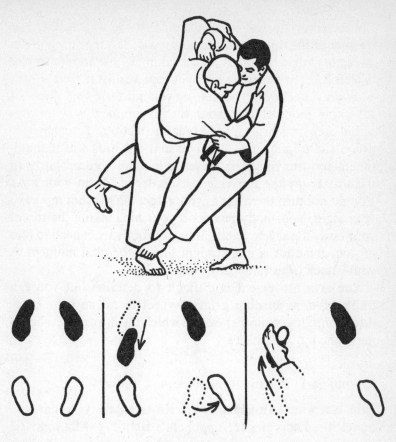

Illustration 27

The opportunity to use this throw occurs when your
opponent is moving sideways – say to his left. Your object is
to sweep away his right leg just before he replaces it on the
mat having completed his step or as he replaces it on the mat
but before he can put his weight upon it. He commences his
step to his left moving his left foot – you follow taking your
right foot to the right and turning it a little to the right, but
not taking quite such a long step. As he moves his right foot
to his left to complete his pace you follow turning your left

53

foot so that you can bring the sole of the foot against the outside of his right ankle. Keeping your left leg straight you sweep his ankle to his left, either taking it past and in front of his left foot, or sweeping his right foot against his left.

As you sweep with your left leg you must use your arms. At the same moment that your throw commences with your initial step you bring your arms into action. Your left arm drives the opponent to his right and upwards whilst simultaneously your right arm drives to his right and upwards. In the usual way the movement is controlled from your hips. You do not turn them but as your sweeping left foot moves to your right, your body pivots on your hips taking the top of your body to the left. In this way your body from head to toes of your left foot is in a straight line at the vital moment of your attack (*illustration 28*).

The arm movement is difficult to describe but you can think of it as turning a large wheel in an anti-clockwise direction. This is another case in which the illustration should make the movement clear.

Ko-soto-gari (The minor outer reaping throw)

Because when attacking with **Ko-soto-gari** you have to attack the back of your opponent's right leg with your left foot, it is necessary either to wait for him to turn sideways thus bringing his right side close to you or for you to move yourself into an attacking position. As by turning sideways to you the opponent gives you your attacking position I will describe the throw from the more difficult position, when you and he are facing each other in the basic posture.

From this position move your right foot to your left, turning it to your right as you do so. This movement is made from the hip and the knee must be bent and relaxed as the foot is replaced on the mat with your weight over the ball of the foot. How far you move the foot must depend on the position of your opponent. Do not move further than is

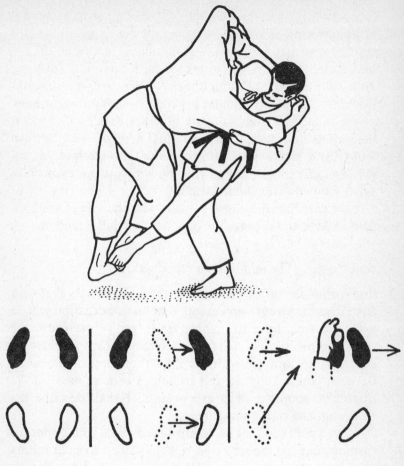

Illustration 28

necessary to make the attack with your left foot because you are bringing your right foot rather close to your left which is a basically weak position. Certainly do not commit the fatal mistake of bringing your right foot across your left thus crossing your feet. The best position for your right foot when it is returned to the mat is about 18 inches (45 cm) in front of the opponent's right foot.

As soon as the right foot is back on the mat bring your left hip and foot forward, and keeping the leg straight place the sole of your left foot behind your opponent's right ankle – just above the heel – and press forward. Simultaneously use your left hand to push him directly downwards aiming your downward drive just behind his right heel. Your right hand pushes against his collar bone downwards also to a point behind his right heel. This is as usual a 'whole body' throw. Your body remains in a straight line, the straight left leg driving against his heel and your body pivoting on your hips driving downwards (*illustration 29*).

Take care that the attack is made with the sole of your left foot. A kick can damage the opponent's achilles tendon.

Ko-uchi-gari (The minor inner reaping throw)

The principle of this throw is very similar to that just described for **Ko-soto-gari** except that on this occasion you do not, as a rule, have to manoeuvre to get yourself into the throwing position. If he is in a defensive posture it may be necessary to move in with the right foot to close the space between you, and in fact this technique is more useful if the opponent adopts a defensive posture. I shall describe the throw against such an opponent.

Move your right foot – and hip – in towards your opponent turning your right foot to your right as you do so and bending your knee. As you do this pull him with your right hand to his left and lift a little. Your left hand pulls him slightly towards you and also lifts. The object is to prevent him stepping backwards to escape from your attack and to enable you to slip your body between his arms as you attack with your left foot.

Your left leg is brought between his feet and the sole of your left foot placed behind his left heel. You now drive his left leg forward with your left foot and with your arms and body drive him downwards to the mat. The drive of your

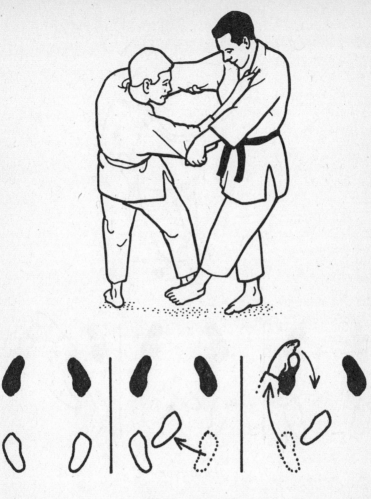

Illustration 29

arms is aimed at the mat just behind his left heel (*illustration 30*).

The drive must be made towards the mat behind his left heel. If you just push downwards equally behind both of his feet he will be able to step back with his right foot and escape. Take great care to keep your balance – otherwise you might

Illustration 30

fall on him and cause injury. The throw can take your opponent clean off the mat (*illustration 31*) and like **O-soto-gari** can be very violent.

Illustration 31

SUTEMI-WAZA (SACRIFICE THROWS AND TECHNIQUES)

The name of this group accurately describes the throws. Sacrifice throws are throws in which you throw yourself – actually sacrifice your own upright posture – in order to defeat your opponent. **Sutemi-waza** are divided into two groups. Those in which you throw yourself on to your back (**Ma-sutemi-waza**) and throws in which you throw yourself on your side (**Yoko-sutemi-waza**).

Tomoe-nage (The stomach or circle throw)

In this technique you throw yourself to your back. Care must be taken because when you are learning there is a danger of kicking your opponent in the stomach and in addition the fall can be very heavy.

The opportunity to attack with this throw occurs when

59

your opponent crouches in a defensive posture holding you out with stiff arms. If he pushes you or can be persuaded to do so it will be easier to make the throw. Assume then that he adopts this position. For this throw you have to get under his defensive arms by lowering your body and pushing his arms upwards. Bending your right knee and using your arms to draw your opponent forward and upward, slide your left foot along the mat until it is between his feet. As you do so curl up your body, tucking in your head. When your left foot is in position sit down on the mat as close as possible to your left heel and still drawing your opponent to his front roll backwards. He will be somersaulted forwards. To avoid him falling on top of you, as you begin to roll back bring your right foot, with the knee bent, up into your opponent's stomach. If your toes are more or less on the knot of his belt your foot is correctly positioned. This foot is not intended to add force to the throw so on no account should you kick or even straighten your right leg. All it does is prevent him falling on top of you and guides his body in the correct circular fall over your body (*illustration 32*). The position is rather like a wheel in which your bottom on the mat is the hub, your right foot a spoke and his body the rim.

I emphasize, your right foot is nothing more than one of the spokes which guide the rim in the correct direction. The spoke should neither shorten nor lengthen – that is, you should not straighten your leg – otherwise the throw must fail and you may well find yourself being held down. I advise the use of a crash mat.

Variation to **Tomoe-nage** (The circle throw)
Whilst the basic throw is easy in theory, in practice an experienced opponent would consider that he has a very good chance of avoiding it and even of holding you down as he does so. Many leading judo contestants change the direction of the throw. As the opponent is going over he turns towards one side and throws him sideways. They continue to turn

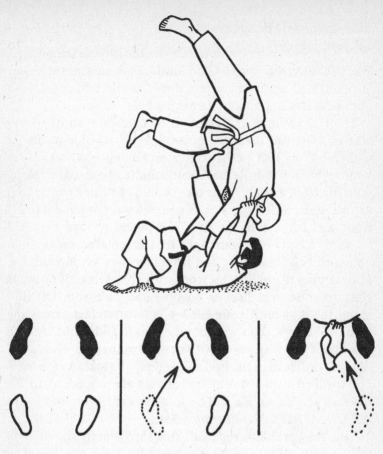

Illustration 32

until they are in a position to apply a hold-down. For example, the thrower decides to turn towards his left as his opponent reaches a position above him thus making the throw to his left. He continues to turn to his left maintaining his grip on the opponent's jacket with his left hand and bringing the right hand round his opponent's neck. He is now in a perfect position to apply **Kesa-gatame** (the scarf hold) shown on page 69.

Yoko-gake (Side body throw)

This is a sacrifice throw in which you throw yourself on your side (**Yoko-sutemi-waza**). Care must be taken, as if the throw is performed badly there is a considerable danger of your opponent landing on and damaging his shoulder.

The real value of the throw is to overcome an opponent who is in a strong defensive posture, as usual holding you out with his arms and perhaps in a crouching position. Move your right foot a little backwards and to your right taking your hip back as well. Your foot should be turned to your left as you replace it on the mat. If you pull your opponent to his front and lift a little as your hip moves he will be tilted forward slightly. As your right foot is replaced on the mat you must bend that knee and withdraw your left hip and leg. Maintaining the pull to his front with your arms, sit down as close to your right heel as possible and slide your left foot along the mat until your left leg is outstretched across the front of his legs. You will find it easier to slide your leg into position if you turn your foot sideways so that the left edge of the foot rather than the heel slides along the mat. As the leg is outstretched turn to your left driving the opponent to his front as you do so. He will be somersaulted over your leg to fall at your left side (*illustration 33*).

You may still succeed with this throw even should you fail to trap your opponent's legs with your left leg. The important point is the outstretching of the leg correctly and the constant driving of the opponent to his front by the continued turn to your left of your body. This turn continues until you are actually on your left side as he falls.

Maki-komi (The winding throw)

This is certainly the most effective throw I used in my contests. As a rule I used it as the second attack in a series (**Renraku-waza**).

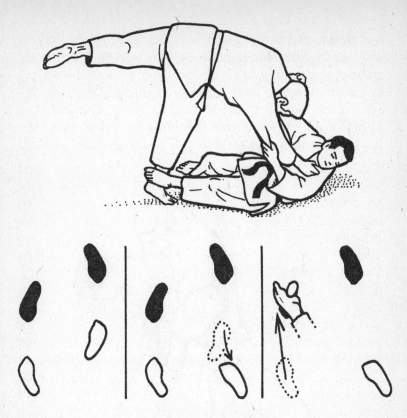

Illustration 33

An extremely effective means of breaking an opponent's defensive posture, this is a difficult throw which can result in a counter attack to your rear. Badly performed it can also result in a severe injury to your opponent's shoulder.

The throw is best made if your opponent has advanced his right foot or can be persuaded by movement on your part to do so. From this position pull hard to your opponent's front with your hands, particularly your left, and withdraw your left foot and hip in a circular movement to your rear and left replacing the foot, turned to the left, about 12 inches (30 cm) in front of his left foot. The knee must be bent with your knee and balanced well over your toes. Without any break in your movement slide your right foot out to your right across the front of your opponent's legs. Your right foot must be turned so that the back of your knee is uppermost (*illustration 34*). This is very similar to the body drop throw, **Tai-otoshi** (*see page 27*). As you commence the throw by withdrawing your left hip you must release the grip of your right hand and take

Illustration 34

your right arm in a circular movement up and to your left bringing it round his right upper arm from above close to his shoulder. You will find it convenient to grip the underside of his sleeve.

At this stage continue your turn clockwise, bending the left knee even more, allowing your right side to drop to the mat. It is essential that you continue the circle round your left hip and do not push the opponent away from you. If you continue to turn and wind him round your body he will fall to his back at your right side (*illustration 35*). The turn must

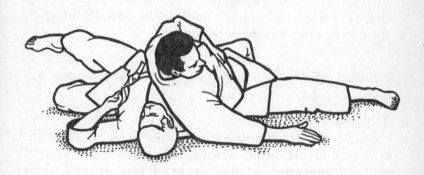

Illustration 35

continue until he falls to the mat and you are almost on your back. You must be beside him when you land on the mat. Never actually fall on his body because this is extremely dangerous. You should have practised often enough to make sure this does not happen or that he does not fall on his shoulder before you attempt the throw in **Randori**. Both these mistakes occur because you fail to continue your turn until your opponent falls or you try to force him down to the mat with your arms. I advise the use of a crash mat.

If you do not score a full point (**Ippon**, *see page 9*) with this throw you should find yourself in a very good position to try for a hold down such as the scarf hold (**Kesa-gatame**) shown on page 69.

RENRAKU-WAZA (CONTINUATION THROWS)

If your throw is a good one, even though it fails, in his efforts to avoid it your opponent is almost certain to give you the opening for a second attack. It is essential that to ensure the success of the second attack you maintain the control of your opponent which you obtained for your initial throwing attempt. This second attempt is a continuation of the first – a **Renraku-waza** – and must be made in the direction in which the opponent is resisting or moving.

Tai-otoshi (Body drop throw) to Harai-goshi (Sweeping hip throw)

You attack with **Tai-otoshi** (*page 27*) but your opponent manages to escape by stepping over your outstretched right foot with his right foot. Maintain the forward and upward pull with your arms and raising your right leg reap backwards with your hip and thigh to throw him with **Harai-goshi** (the sweeping hip throw *page 37*).

Tai-otoshi (Body drop throw) to O-soto-gari (Major outer reaping throw) or O-uchi-gari (Major inner reaping throw)

You attack with **Tai-otoshi** (*page 27*) but the throw fails because your opponent manages to throw his balance backwards. Maintain your pull to his front but pivot to your right on your left foot and bring your right heel behind his right knee. Now throw him by pulling his right leg towards you and by driving your body forward from your hips – that is to his rear. Use your arms to thrust down towards the mat just behind his right heel. Although you are not sufficiently close for the true version this is **O-soto-gari** (the major outer reaping throw *page 30*).

Sometimes you cannot reach his right leg with your right leg. In this case it may be possible, or easier, to bring your right foot between his legs and behind his left knee. The throw (**O-uchi-gari**) follows the same lines as **O-soto-gari** except that you drive him down behind his left heel.

Harai-goshi (Sweeping hip throw) to **Maki-komi** (The winding throw)

You attempt **Harai-goshi,** the sweeping hip throw (*page 37*), but your opponent manages to resist it. Maintain the pull of your arms to his front and slightly upwards and then, releasing your grip on his jacket with your right hand, bring your right arm up and over his right arm taking a grip on his right sleeve on the underside. At the same time slide your right leg out to your right and turn your head, shoulders and hips to your left. Continue your turn until you drop to your right side. Your opponent will be thrown on his back at your side with **Maki-komi** (*page 62*). As you commence your turn to throw with **Maki-komi** you must bend your left knee. The more deeply you bend the knee the more effective and easy the throw.

NE-WAZA (GROUNDWORK OR GROUND TECHNIQUES)

Groundwork consists of three sections. Holding techniques, neck locks which involve attacks on your opponent's breathing or blood supply and finally arm locks which are applied to the elbow. As neck and arm locks are dangerous for beginners and juniors they are not included in this book. Not only are young people's bodies not fully developed but juniors may not appreciate the dangerous consequences of the technique they are attempting. This leaves us with the hold down techniques which by themselves require many years' study to acquire real proficiency.

To obtain a hold (**Osaekomi**) you have to pin your opponent on his back. Once the hold is recognized by the referee's call of '**Osaekomi**' it does not matter whether the opponent remains completely on his back; he may roll over on to one shoulder – provided you maintain control over him.

OSAEKOMI-WAZA (HOLDING TECHNIQUES) BASIC PRINCIPLES

There are a few principles which apply to all holds:

1 The whole body must always be relaxed.

2 The main weight of the attacker's body should be on the mat – not on his opponent. In this way his balance is not disturbed by his opponent's struggles.

3 Once the hold has been applied, the attacker must maintain the same relative position between himself and his opponent. He must therefore follow every move his opponent makes. In this way his balance and therefore his hold is not broken.

4 The attacker's posture on the mat should be both balanced and flexible. His body should act as a tripod, the three legs of which are his two legs and his hips all of which should be kept well spread and on the mat. If the person being held can manoeuvre so that he can persuade the holder to bring any two legs of the tripod too close together, the tripod will collapse. That is to say the hold can be broken.

5 Never attempt to continue with a hold once you have begun to lose control. Change to another hold or break away as soon as possible otherwise your opponent is likely to be able to reverse the position and hold you.

6 It is important that you use your arms to pull your opponent towards your hips and your hips are firmly positioned on the mat. This locks his body making escape very difficult.

These principles will become clear when you read the description of the holds and look at the illustrations but above all try out the holds on the mat. You will find that you will develop variations of your own depending on your physique.

SUBMISSION

Although it is usually only necessary to submit (that is give up) to arm and neck locks it does happen that you wish to make your opponent release a hold down. Perhaps the pressure he is exerting is too great or you have a hand trapped in his jacket. The formal submission is to tap twice on his body with your hand or on the mat with either hand or foot. However the main thing is that he does understand that you submit and releases the hold. Therefore make your submission absolutely clear – shout if necessary. From the other point of view, if you are holding release your hold immediately on a submission, and should you be in any doubt as to whether he has or has not submitted, play it safe and let go.

OSAEKOMI-WAZA (HOLDING TECHNIQUES)
Kesa-gatame (The scarf hold)

Your opponent is on his back and you are at his right side. Sit on the mat close to his right side and slide your right arm round his neck to grip the back of his jacket underneath his right shoulder. The arm goes round like a scarf, hence the name of the throw. Now, sitting on your right thigh, push your right knee up by your opponent's right ear and throw your leg forward from the knee. Your left leg is thrown back, from the knee. Your body is now spread like a tripod, the three legs being your two feet and right thigh on which you are sitting. The right side of your body should be pressed against the right side of his ribs (*illustration 36*).

Illustration 36

I have left my description of the most important part of this hold – his right arm – to the end. With your left hand grip his sleeve close to his right shoulder. His right arm should be trapped between your arm, your right thigh and your stomach. Pull his arm hard and steadily towards your armpit and finally tuck your head down so that he cannot get his left hand under your chin to push you back.

To prevent your opponent breaking the hold you must:

1 Keep the weight of your hips on the mat. It is fatal to lift your hips and place your weight on your opponent.

2 Keep your right knee close to your opponent's ear and your left leg thrown back.

3 Maintain this position at all costs no matter how hard your opponent struggles. As he moves round follow him.

Kuzure-kesa-gatame (The broken scarf hold)

This hold is very similar to **Kesa-gatame**. The only difference is the position of the right hand which instead of going under your opponent's neck is placed between his left side and left arm (*illustration 37*). Usually the right hand is placed palm down on the mat. Many people consider that this hold is more flexible than **Kesa-gatame**. Not only can the right arm be moved to aid your balance, especially should he attempt to roll you over his body, but having it free makes it easier for you to change from this hold to another should you wish to do so.

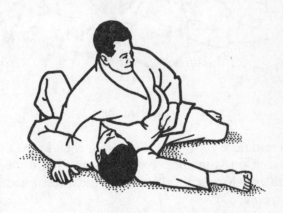

Illustration 37

Kata-gatame (The shoulder hold)

Although this hold can be applied at any time the opportunity usually occurs when you are attempting **Kesa-gatame** from your opponent's right side and he, in an effort to escape, manages to free, or partly free, his right arm. As he does so release your grip on it and push it to his left so that it lies

71

across his neck (*illustration 38*). Place the right side of your face and head against the outside of his arm and press his arm into his neck. You clasp your hands together behind his right shoulder. As you commence to press his right arm across his neck pivot on your hips by bringing your left leg across your

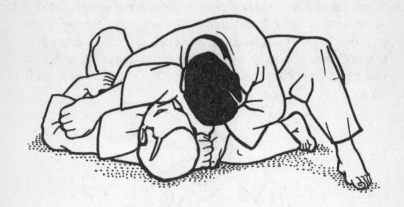

Illustration 38

right and raise your body up on your right knee. Your left leg is braced on your toes. From this position drive your hips down and forward to maintain the pressure on his arm (*illustration 39*).

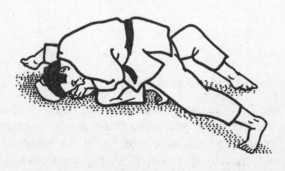

Illustration 39

Like all movements in judo the key to this hold is the pivot of your hips and then the pressure exerted as you press forward and downward with the hips obtaining the pressure from the toes of your left foot.

Kami-shiho-gatame (The upper four quarter hold)

There are several variations to this hold all of which are equally effective. The hold described is the basic version. Your opponent is on his back on the ground and you are positioned close to his head; certainly level with his shoulders and too high up to apply **Kesa-gatame**. Placing yourself face downwards grip his belt with your arms against his body, and your elbows pressing up into his armpits. With your hands as far back as possible on his belt, certainly touching the mat, pull upwards towards you. Your head is turned sideways and is pressed down on his chest (*illustration 40*). Do not work your way too far down his body – your hips must be pressing down on the mat above his head and your legs spread wide apart, your toes pressing against the mat. We have the basic tripod here again – the three legs being your hips and your widely spread feet.

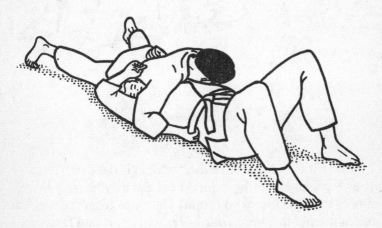

Illustration 40

73

To maintain the hold against a resisting opponent pull your elbows hard up into his armpits in order to exert upward pressure against his shoulders. This reduces the effectiveness of his arms. Use your legs as levers to resist any effort he might make to turn you over and escape.

Variations to **Kami-shiho-gatame**

There are several variations to this hold of which I will describe three:

1 Take your arms round those of your opponent and by gripping his belt as for the basic hold, pin his arms to his side (*illustration 41*).

Illustration 41

2 Hold with your arms in either way but instead of lying with your legs spread bring your knees up to your opponent's shoulders. This forces you to lift your hips from the mat but to counteract this keep your knees well apart and force your hips down (*illustration 42*).

Illustration 42

3 This variation has a name of its own. It is called **Kuzure-kami-shiho-gatame** (the broken upper four quarter hold). The position is much the same as for **Kami-shiho-gatame**. You are face down with your hips on the mat and your legs thrown back well apart. This time you take your left arm under his left armpit and pass it behind his shoulders to grip his jacket beneath his right shoulder (*illustration 43*). The right arm holds his belt as before. You now move so that your hips are above his left shoulder with your right leg more or less in line with his body. It is usual and more comfortable to bend the left leg.

Illustration 43

Yoko-shiho-gatame (The side four quarter hold)

Again your opponent is on his back and you are positioned at his right side. Kneel beside him and bring your left arm behind his neck and grip his jacket behind his left shoulder. Your right arm is taken between his legs and grips the back of his belt. If you cannot reach that far grip the back of his jacket as close to his belt as possible. Now throw your legs back forcing your hips down on to the mat and spreading your legs to form the usual hold down tripod. Alternatively the knees can be drawn up against your opponent's body. Your knees should be well apart so that you can push your hips downward towards the mat. Personally I draw up my left knee. This always feels stronger to me (*illustration 44*).

Illustration 44

Variations to **Yoko-shiho-gatame**
Instead of bringing your right arm between your opponent's legs to grip the back of his belt, take it across his body to hold his jacket close to his left shoulder. Your hands are now holding his jacket quite close to each other (*illustration 45*).

Illustration 45

A further variation is to bring your knees close to the right side of his body. Keep them well apart and force your hips down to the mat. You can use this variation of the leg position however you hold with your hands.

Ushiro-kesa-gatame (The reverse scarf hold)

Your opponent is on his back on the mat and this time you are on his left side. Throw your right arm across his body and pressing your elbow into his right armpit grip his belt close to the mat with your right hand. As a result of these movements you are now reclining on your right hip with your right leg thrown forward along your opponent's left side. Your left leg is thrown back as in **Kesa-gatame** (*illustration 46*). Your right hip and your feet form the tripod in this hold. With your left arm you trap his left arm between your upper arm and body, gripping his jacket close to the armpit. To secure your position tuck your head down on to his chest and throw your left leg back from the knee.

Illustration 46

MAINTAINING HOLDS AGAINST RESISTANCE

Naturally your opponent will not be prepared to remain held without making strenuous efforts to escape. To maintain your hold you must remain relaxed and prevent your opponent disturbing the relative position between you and him. As he moves in his attempts to escape you move with him. It is unwise to fight to retain your hold once you have begun to lose control. The most effective action is to change to another hold down. For example if you are using **Kesa-gatame** (*page 69*) and your opponent begins to escape, by turning your hips clockwise so that you are face down on the mat you can easily change your position into **Kami-shiho-gatame** (*page 73*). From here to **Kuzuri-kami-shiho-gatame** is only a matter of changing the position of your left arm and moving your body a little. From this position a change to **Ushiro-kesa-gatame** (*page 77*) is fairly simple and a further change to **Yoko-shiho-gatame** (*page 76*) at your opponent's left side is a possibility. Playing at changing from hold to hold with a co-operative partner is excellent practice.

METHODS OF BREAKING HOLDS ON THE GROUND

If a hold is applied correctly and no mistake is made it should not be broken unless considerably greater strength is available, but by taking positive and immediate action as soon as you are held you can often induce your opponent to give you the opportunity you require. Although I shall only describe two methods of breaking **Kesa-gatame** (*page 69*) the principles apply to all ground holds.

Methods of breaking **Kesa-gatame** (the scarf hold)

1 You are being held in **Kesa-gatame,** your right arm being pinned by your opponent. The first essential is to free that arm. To do this brace your left foot against the mat and pull your right hip, shoulder and arm away from your opponent (*illustration 47*). The move must be sudden and strong. It is

Illustration 47

only necessary to move your arm about 2 inches (5 cm). Immediately, or perhaps before you do this, bring your body close to that of your opponent and reaching across him with your left arm grip his left sleeve as close to the end as possible.

At this stage you should be on your right side. Using the upward leverage of your right arm against his chest and the pull of your left arm, pull him into you and maintaining this pull turn your hips and body hard to your left (anti-clockwise). This time the drive should be made from the pressure of your right foot on the mat. If you move correctly he will be rolled over your body to the mat at your left side (*illustration 48*). Now you can apply a hold down on him.

Illustration 48

2 Again you are being held with **Kesa-gatame,** your opponent being at your right side and controlling your right arm. The basic movement to escape is very much as just described. You must pull your right hip and shoulder away from him and obtain a little freedom for your right arm. Continue this anti-clockwise turning movement, pulling with your right arm and driving from your left foot bring your left hand between his head and your own. You should attempt to press the palm of this hand flat down on the mat, using this movement to assist your turn (*illusration 49*). You should find that the turn of your hips and right arm added to the downward thrust of

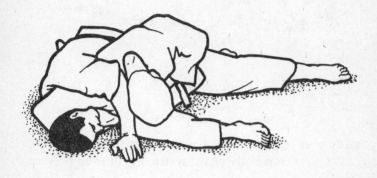

Illustration 49

your left hand and arm should enable you to pull your head and shoulders free of his controlling right arm. The hold is then completely broken and you can escape or counter attack. The opportunity for an armlock is obvious (*illustration 50*).

Space is not available to describe the twenty or so other methods of breaking **Kesa-gatame** but I hope the two shown will provide some idea of the methods which can be used. The other holds can be counter attacked in much the same way. It is useless to attempt one method and, should that fail, try another. The idea is to counter attack immediately a hold is attempted against you. The various escape methods should be used continuously without a break, one being changed to another as your opponent moves to counter your efforts. One thing you must remember is that you will never escape a hold unless you use both hands and your hips and attempt to

Illustration 50

control your opponent's movement. The object is to be able
to move your own body whilst restricting or even preventing
his movement.

FINDING AND JOINING A CLUB

Not only do you have to find a club but you have to find a
good one. The first essential is that it must be a member of
your National Association, in Britain the British Judo
Association. If you have any doubt about this ask your
Olympic Association which judo association it recognizes.
Should you live in or near a town you may find that you have
a choice of several clubs. In this case I suggest you visit them
and watch the instruction. If you like the way the club is
organized and the nature of the teaching it is probably the
club for you. However always look at two or three clubs if
they are available and if possible see what you can find out
about their reputation in the judo world. Consider the fees
but these do not always relate to the facilities and instruction
offered. Certainly it is worth travelling an extra distance to
attend a better club.

Do not be tempted to buy a judo suit (**Judogi**) before you join your club because as a rule the club will charge you far less for the same or similar items.

What then should you expect to pay when you decide to start judo? Most clubs and schools charge a joining fee and an annual subscription. In addition you must expect to pay a small fee each time you attend for instruction. You will also be expected to have your own judo suit. This may sound expensive but if you compare it with the cost of most other sports you will find it cheaper than most, especially when you consider that qualified supervision and instruction will be available at all times. However do make sure that this form of instruction is always available – it is not unknown for some teachers to hand over to one of their students.

When you first walk into the **Dojo** (training hall) of a club you will see that judo is practised in bare feet and anyone leaving the mat immediately puts on a pair of slippers. Proper judo slippers are called **Zori**. This is to prevent dirt picked up from the floor being carried on to the mat. The very young members (most clubs accept junior members from the age of 6) may well be playing games connected with judo but most will be working very hard attempting techniques under the direction of a teacher or attempting to throw or hold each other.

Judo is not easy to learn and it is therefore easy to become discouraged. However large the club you join your practice will be limited to a comparatively limited number of fellow students. As you learn each other's methods and favourite techniques you will find that your attacks are frequently blocked. The answer to this is not to become discouraged and give up but rather to look for the reason for your failure and find a method of succeeding with the technique. In this way you will progress in skill and in grade.

If you already practise judo no doubt you will learn from this book. If you are a newcomer I hope it has interested you sufficiently for you to find a club and take part in the sport. I wish you every success in your judo career and can only hope it brings you as much pleasure and excitement as it did – and still does – to me.

List of terms used in judo

An asterisk indicates that the technique is included in this book.

THROWS

Ashi-guruma   Leg wheel throw
*__Ashi-waza__   Leg and foot techniques
De-ashi-barai   Advanced foot sweep throw
Hane-goshi   Spring hip throw
Hane-makikomi   Winding spring hip throw
*__Harai-goshi__   Sweeping hip or loin throw
Harai-tsurikomi-ashi   Sweeping drawing ankle throw
*__Hiza-guruma__   Knee wheel throw
*__Ippon-seoi-nage__   One sided shoulder throw
Kata-guruma   Shoulder wheel throw
Koshi-guruma   Hip or loin wheel throw
*__Koshi-waza__   Hip or loin techniques
Ko-soto-gake   Minor outer hook throw
*__Ko-soto-gari__   Minor outer reaping throw
*__Ko-uchi-gari__   Minor inner reaping throw
*__Maki-komi__   Winding throw
*__Ma-sutemi-waza__   Technique in which the attacker throws
   himself on his back to make the throw
*__Morote-seoi-nage__   Two sided shoulder throw
*__O-goshi__   Major hip throw
O-guruma   Major wheel throw
*__Okuri-ashi-barai__   Sweeping ankle throw
*__O-soto-gari__   Major outer reaping throw
O-soto-gaeshi   Turning **O-soto-gari** throw

O-soto-guruma   Side wheel throw

*****O-uchi-gari**   Major inner reaping throw

*****Randori**   Free practice

*****Renraku-waza**   Combination throw technique

*****Sasae-tsurikomi-ashi**   Lifting drawing ankle throw

*****Seoi-nage**   Shoulder throw

*****Seoi-otoshi**   Shoulder drop throw

*****Seoi-waza**   Shoulder throw technique

  Soto-makikomi   Outer winding throw

  Suki-nage   Scooping throw

  Sumi-gaeshi   Corner throw

  Sumi-ogoshi   Corner drop throw

*****Sutemi-waza**   Sacrifice throw techniques

*****Tachi-waza**   Standing or throwing techniques

*****Tai-otoshi**   Body drop throw

  Tani-otoshi   Valley drop throw

  Te-guruma   Hand throw technique

*****Tomoe-nage**   Stomach or circle throw

  Tsuri-goshi   Lifting hip throw

  Tsuki-komi-ashi   Drawing ankle throw

*****Tsuki-komi-goshi**   Lifting drawing hip throw

*****Uchi-mata**   Inner thigh throw

*****Ukemi**   Breaking your fall

  Uki-goshi   Floating hip throw

  Uki-otoshi   Floating drop throw

  Uki-waza   Floating throw technique

  Ura-nage   Rear throw

  Ushiro-goshi   Rear hip or loin throw

  Utsuru-goshi   Changing hip throw

*****Yama-arashi**   Mountain storm throw

*****Yoko-gake**   Side body drop throw

  Yoko-guruma   Side wheel throw

  Yoko-otoshi   Side drop throw

  Yoko-wakare   Side separation throw

HOLDING TECHNIQUES

*Kami-shiho-gatame   Upper four quarter hold
*Kata-gatame   Shoulder hold
*Kesa-gatame   Scarf hold
*Kuzure-kami-shiho-gatame   Broken upper four quarter hold
*Kuzure-kesa-gatame   Broken scarf hold
 Kuzure-tate-shiho-gatame   Broken lengthways hold
 Kuzure-yoko-shiho-gatame   Broken side four quarter hold
 Makura-kesa-gatame   Pillow scarf hold
 Mune-gatame   Chest hold
*Ne-waza   Groundwork techniques
*Osaekomi-waza   Holding techniques
 Tate-shiho-gatame   Lengthways hold
*Ushiro-kesa-gatame   Reverse scarf hold
*Yoko-shiho-gatame   Side four quarter hold

REFEREES CALLS AND INSTRUCTIONS

Chui   A penalty worth 5 points to opponent
Hajime   Start. Commence the contest
Hansoku   Disqualification. Penalty worth 10 points to opponent
Hantei   Referee's call to judges at end of a drawn contest for their decision
Ippon (Ipon)   Point. A score. Win by a clean throw, hold down or submission. Worth 10 points
Ippon-sogo-gachi   Win by **Ippon** made up by **Waza-ari** (7 points) plus **Keikoku** against opponent (7 points)
Jikan   Referee's instruction to time keeper during contest to deduct time
Keikoku   A penalty worth 7 points to opponent

Koka   A score worth 3 points. Almost a **Yuko**

Matte   Break, wait

Osaekomi   Holding. A hold down has commenced

Rei   Bow

Shido   Penalty worth 3 points to opponent

Toketa   Hold broken

Waza-ari   Almost **Ippon**. A score worth 7 points

Waza-ari-awesete-ippon   **Ippon** made up by two **Waza-ari**.
   Worth 10 points

Yoshi   Carry on

Yuko   Almost **Waza-ari**. Worth 5 points

GENERAL TERMS

Ashi   Leg, foot

Ashi-waza   Leg or foot technique

Barai   Sweep, reap

Budo   Military arts or ways

Bu-jitsu   Martial arts (all forms)

Butsukari   A method of training in which a throw is taken
   to the final point of balance without being actually made

Dan   Advanced grade. Black belt holder

De   To advance (*see* **De-ashi-barai)**

Do   The way or path (*see* **Judo)**

Dojo   Martial arts practice hall

Eri   Collar of jacket

Fusegu   To defend

Gake   To hook or block

Gaeshi   To counter

Garami   To entangle, bend

Goshi   Hip (*see* **Harai-goshi)**

Guruma   Wheel (*see* **Ashi-guruma)**

Gyaku   Reverse

Hadaka   Naked

Hane   Spring

Hara   Stomach

Harai   Sweep, reap

Hidari   Left

Hishigi   To crush

Hiza   Knee (*see* **Hiza-guruma**)

Hon   Basic

Jigotai   Defensive posture

Joseki   The place in the **Dojo** occupied by the seniors or honoured guests

Ju   Soft, gentle

Judogi   Judo clothing

Judoka   A person who practises judo of at least 4th Dan grade

Kaeshi   To counter

Kaeshi-waza   Counter techniques

Kake   The point in a throw at which the maximum power is applied

Kai (or **Kwai**)   Society or club

Kansetsu   A joint

Kansetsu-waza   Joint locking techniques

Kata   1 An arranged set of techniques designed to develop the performance, posture, balance and technique

2 One side

3 Shoulder (*see* **Kata-gatame**)

Keiko   Practice

Kiai   A shout used to obtain maximum power

Ko   Small, minor (*see* **Ko-soto-gari**)

Koshi   Hip (*see* **Koshi-waza**)

Kuzure   Broken (*see* **Kuzure-kesa-gatame**)

Kyu   The student grade

Mae   Front

Maitta   I give up

Migi   Right (opposite to left)

Mon   Gate, junior grade

Morote   Both hands (*see* **Morote-seoi-nage**)

Nage   To throw (*see* **Nage-waza**)

Nage-no-kate   A means to training in which 15 throws are performed in a set sequence

Nage-waza   Throwing techniques

Ne-waza   Groundwork techniques

O   Big, major (*see* **O-goshi**)

Obi   Belt

Osaekomi-waza   Holding techniques

Otoshi   To drop (*see* **Tai-otoshi**)

Randori   Free practice

Rei   Bow

Sensei   Master, senior teacher

Seoi   To carry (*see* **Ippon-seoi-nage**)

Shiai   Contest

Shiaijo   Contest area

Shihan   Master, pastmaster

Shiho   Four quarters or directions (*see* **Yoko-shiho-gatame**)

Soto   Outside (*see* **O-soto-gari**)

Sukui   To scoop up

Sumi   Corner (*see* **Sumi-gaeshi**)

Sutemi   To throw away (*see* **Sutemi-waza**)

Tachi   To stand (*see* **Tachi-waza**)

Tai   Body (*see* **Tai-otoshi**)

Tatami   Straw mats used in a **Dojo** (nowadays usually made of rubber)

Te   Hand (*see* **Te-waza**)

Tokui   Favourite

Tokui-waza   Favourite throw

Tomoe   To turn over (*see* **Tomoe-nage**)

Tori   The person who throws

Tsugi-ashi   A method of walking on the mat in which the same foot leads at each step, the other never passing it

Tsukuri   Breaking the opponent's balance

Tsuri   To lift (*see* **Tsuri-komi**)

Uchikomi An exercise in which the throwing technique is taken just to the point of throwing

Ude Arm

Ukemi The breakfall

Uki To float (*see* **Uki-otoshi**)

Ura Back to rear (*see* **Ura-nage**)

Ushiro Behind, back (*see* **Ushiro-goshi**)

Yama Mountain (*see* **Yama-arashi**)

Yoko Side (*see* **Yoko-shiho-gatame**)

Waza Technique

Zori Straw sandals worn off the mat (nowadays usually made of rubber)